JAMES

THE IMPLANTED WORD

8 INTERACTIVE BIBLE STUDIES FOR
SMALL GROUPS AND INDIVIDUALS

PHILLIP D JENSEN
AND KIRSTEN BIRKETT

matthiasmedia
SYDNEY · YOUNGSTOWN

Matthias Media
(St Matthias Press Ltd ACN 067 558 365)
Email: info@matthiasmedia.com.au
Internet: www.matthiasmedia.com.au
Please visit our website for current postal and telephone contact information.

Matthias Media (USA)
Email: sales@matthiasmedia.com
Internet: www.matthiasmedia.com
Please visit our website for current postal and telephone contact information.

ISBN 978 1 921441 81 3

Cover design and typesetting by Matthias Media.
Series concept design by Lankshear Design.

» CONTENTS

» HOW TO MAKE THE MOST OF THESE STUDIES

1. What is an Interactive Bible Study?

Interactive Bible Studies are a bit like a guided tour of a famous city. They take you through a particular part of the Bible, helping you to know where to start, pointing out things along the way, suggesting avenues for further exploration, and making sure that you know how to get home. Like any good tour, the real purpose is to allow you to go exploring for yourself—to dive in, have a good look around, and discover for yourself the riches that God's word has in store.

In other words, these studies aim to provide stimulation and input and point you in the right direction, while leaving you to do plenty of the exploration and discovery yourself.

We hope that these studies will stimulate lots of 'interaction'—interaction with the Bible, with the things we've written, with your own current thoughts and attitudes, with other people as you discuss them, and with God as you talk to him about it all.

2. The format

The studies contain five main components:

- sections of text that introduce, inform, summarize and challenge
- numbered questions that help you examine the passage and think through its meaning
- sidebars that provide extra bits of background or optional extra study ideas, especially regarding other relevant parts of the Bible
- 'Implications' sections that help you think about what this passage means for you and your life today
- suggestions for thanksgiving and prayer as you close.

3. How to use these studies on your own

- Before you begin, pray that God would open your eyes to what he is saying in the Bible, and give you the spiritual strength to do something about it.
- Work through the study, reading the text, answering the questions about the Bible passage, and exploring the sidebars as you have time.
- Resist the temptation to skip over the 'Implications' and 'Give thanks and pray' sections at the end. It is important that we not only hear and understand God's word, but respond to it. These closing sections help us do that.
- Take what opportunities you can to talk to others about what you've learnt.

4. How to use these studies in a small group

- Much of the above applies to group study as well. The studies are suitable for structured Bible study or cell groups, as well as for more informal pairs and triplets. Get together with a friend or friends and work through them at your own pace; use them as the basis for regular Bible study with your spouse. You don't need the formal structure of a 'group' to gain maximum benefit.

- For small groups, it is very useful if group members can work through the study themselves before the group meets. The group discussion can take place comfortably in an hour (depending on how sidetracked you get!) if all the members have done some work in advance.
- The role of the group leader is to direct the course of the discussion and to try to draw the threads together at the end. This will mean a little extra preparation— underlining the sections of text to emphasize and read out loud, working out which questions are worth concentrating on, and being sure of the main thrust of the study. Leaders will also probably want to work out approximately how long they'd like to spend on each part.
- If your group members usually don't work through the study in advance, it's extra important that the leader prepares which parts to concentrate on, and which parts to glide past more quickly. In particular, the leader will need to select which of the 'Implications' to focus on.
- We haven't included an 'answer guide' to the questions in the studies. This is a deliberate move. We want to give you a guided tour of the Bible, not a lecture. There is more than enough in the text we have written and the questions we have asked to point you in what we think is the right direction. The rest is up to you.

5. Bible translation

Previous editions of this Interactive Bible Study have assumed that most readers would be using the New International Version of the Bible. However, since the release of the English Standard Version in 2001, many have switched to the ESV for study purposes. So with this new edition of *The Implanted Word*, we have decided to quote from and refer to the ESV text, which we recommend. There should not generally be any problems, however, if you are using a different translation. (Nevertheless, it might be useful to have an ESV on hand in case of any confusion.)

A FIRST LOOK AT JAMES

[OVERVIEW]

Whoever wishes to be a friend of the world makes himself an enemy of God. (Jas 4:4)

STRONG WORDS FROM JAMES! No complicated theoretical arguments here—James gets right to the point and tells us what to do. This is what most people love about James. The advice it gives on behaviour is easy to understand and speaks directly to everyday life. You could discuss the practical issues for hours. You want to live a Christian life? This is how you do it.

There is a lot more to James, however, than snippets of good advice. When you read James for the first time (or even the 20th) it can seem very disjointed. Lots of sensible suggestions, you might think, but what holds them together? Does anything? Or is this just a general collection of wise sayings?

There is a basic theme that holds the whole of James together, and we hope that this will become clear as you work through these studies. James was not just writing a little handbook of sayings. He was applying God's wisdom to common difficulties in Christian living. James teaches that true knowledge of God is much more than knowing things about God, for if you do not put your knowledge into action, you do not really know God at all.

James is tremendously encouraging to study, for it challenges us to rethink our commitment to Christ. We hope that James will spur you on in your Christian life, as God reveals his way to you.

What are the main themes?

FIRST OF ALL WE NEED TO GET A FEEL for the *kind* of book we're studying. Having a better appreciation of the biblical background to the book, its original readership and its author, will help us understand the particular statements when we get to them.

Read all of James.

1. Fill in this table.

Chapter	Theme	Key words
1	joy in suffering	trials, persevere
2		
3		
4		
5		

2. Is there a main idea that you think dominates the letter?

Answer the following questions by skimming back through the whole book. (If you have a group of ten or more people, you could break into five groups of two or more and have each group read one chapter.)

3. What elements of the gospel can you find? For instance, what references are there to the following?

- Jesus

- God's election

- salvation by the Word

- responses to salvation:
    - faith

    - humility

- preservation and endurance of Christians

- final consequences

4. What was happening in the church to which James was writing? (E.g. 4:1 indicates they were fighting.)

THIS LETTER HAS OFTEN BEEN described as having a 'Jewish' flavour. Indeed, you may have noticed as you read through James that there is not much mention of Jesus, the gospel, the cross and other Christian ideas you may expect. The Christian theology, however, is definitely there. The letter concentrates mostly on the practical out-working of that theology; but as **James** reminds us, real theology requires practical outworking.

People sometimes have difficulties with James. These are some of the common difficulties:

- There seems to be no structure, no common thread holding the ideas together.
- What James says about faith and works seems to be different from what Paul says (for instance in Romans 1-3).
- What does it mean when it talks about healing by prayer?

We will be tackling these problems as we work through the letter, section by section.

We could probably sum up the book with James' command in 1:21-22: "receive with meekness the implanted word, which is able to save your souls. But be doers of the word, and not hearers only…" We have here a letter written to people who were struggling under the pressures of living in a fallen world; and the solution is to humbly accept God's wisdom found in God's word. James reinforces this message with many practical examples that will hit us hard. When we read the book of James carefully, we will see it is not a hotchpotch of wise sayings after all, but a firm challenge to live by the divinely implanted Word in the trials and difficulties of the real world.

Who was James?

There are probably five different men called James in the New Testament. Three were apostles (the son of Zebedee, the son of Alphaeus and the brother of Jesus); there is also the brother of Jude mentioned in Jude 1; and the father of the Apostle Judas (not Iscariot). We do not know which one wrote the letter James. The good news is that we can still understand God's word regardless of whether we have this outside knowledge. We know from the book in front of us that James is a Christian, a servant of God and Christ (1:1) and a teacher (3:1). That is all we need to know about him.

» Give thanks and pray

- Thank God for giving us his word, which helps us to know him better and to know how we are to act in this world as his children.
- Ask God to help you understand his word as you read and study James.
- Pray that you will be "doers of the word, and not hearers only".

ACTING IN ADVERSITY

[JAMES 1:1-18]

Shannon, by God's grace, became a Christian. Unfortunately, she did not understand much doctrine. She just knew that she wanted to give her life to Christ. Her friends who had explained the gospel to her had not tried to hide anything—they were just overwhelmed with the love of Christ, and had convinced her that being a Christian was the best way to live.

The first time Shannon heard a sermon on suffering as a Christian, she thought it was a bit heavy. After all, if being a Christian is the best way to live, how can it involve suffering? But the issue of suffering kept appearing in sermons. As she looked at the Bible more closely, it became obvious that Christians there suffered—and moreover, that the Bible taught overtly that Christians should expect to suffer. She began to feel terribly afraid, and even began to mistrust God. If this was what God wanted for Christians, what was he going to do to her? Far from the joy in life that she first felt in being a Christian, Shannon began to dread the future.

How do we come to terms with the reality that Christians will suffer? Is it possible still to be thankful to God, even when he sends us trials? If you are not facing any suffering at the moment, it may be easy for you to think about how to cope with trials and even thank God for them. But if you are in the midst of suffering, you know what a desperately important issue this is. We live in a fallen world, and sooner or later we will face hard times. We must understand what suffering accomplishes in our lives, and know how to look to God in suffering, not away from him. It is the old issue of seeing the glass as half full or half empty—how do we see our trials?

Read James 1:1–18.

1. What is the wrong way to respond to trials (e.g. v. 13)?

2. Do you see anything odd about the way in which words are used in verses 1–18? Any apparent paradoxes or contradictions?

Responding to trials

IN THIS PASSAGE THERE IS A PLAY ON the words 'trial' and 'tempt'. A note on translation is useful here. There is a Greek word that has been (rightly) translated as two English words. This is the word that has been translated as "trials" in verses 2 and 12 and "tempted" in verses 13 and 14. Both refer to difficulty that people might face in life. When the difficulty is external, it is called a trial— something that comes to us from outside (e.g. poverty, sickness, oppression, gossip). When we are facing this external difficulty, we may also face an internal difficulty, which we call 'temptation'. If we give in to this internal pressure, we sin. For example, when rich people discriminate against us, we can be tempted to envy or revenge. These sinful thoughts come from within us.

God brings trials, that is, external difficulties. He does it to test us, in the sense of testing or proving metal— making it stronger through fire. He does not bring temptation—that is our own internal and sinful reaction to the difficulties. The two are connected, for within the external difficulty the internal may happen; but if it does, we must not blame God. It is by our own evil desire that we are dragged away and enticed. It is up to us to respond to trials in a godly fashion.

Look back over James 1:1–18.

3. What is the right response to trials?

4. What will be the result of responding in this way (vv. 3-4, 12)?

IT IS DIFFICULT TO SEE HOW TRIALS could ever be "all joy". We may bear them, we may even be able to put on a good face when they come; but trials are most definitely not "all joy". They are painful. That's why we call them 'trials'. So what does James mean?

The key is to look at exactly what the text says. It does not say that trials are, or can be, pure joy; but that we are to consider it pure joy when we face them. How can we do that? We can do it with the wisdom of God, and God will give this wisdom to anyone who asks.

There is a condition, however— when we ask, we must believe and not doubt (v. 6). Does this mean that we have to work ourselves up into a state where we absolutely believe, with not a skerrick of doubt? Verse 6 becomes more understandable when we read on to verse 8 and its description of the doubting man. Is it that he does not know whether God will answer? Is it

that he does not believe God will answer? No; it is that he is a double-minded man. What does that mean?

If we only had this one reference to the double-minded man, we may have been left uncertain; however, this double-mindedness is spoken of again in 4:8, and there it is quite clear what the phrase means. The people in 4:8 are asking for wealth, but so that they may spend money on their pleasures. This is the double-mindedness. To ask is godly, but their motives are entirely ungodly— they are in two minds while asking. The same applies to asking for wisdom in chapter 1. If you are double-minded—if you have ungodly reasons for asking for wisdom—then you cannot expect God to give it to you. He wants you to have wisdom so you can persevere under trials, and so reach maturity. If you ask for any other reason, then you have misunderstood the need for wisdom, and God may not give you what you want.

Facing trials of many kinds

NOW WE CAN MAKE SENSE OF THE paradoxes in James 1:2-18 (such as how trials could be connected with joy). We have joy in trials when we look at them with God's wisdom, and recognize that good will come of these trials no matter how difficult they are now. That does not mean we are masochists and want to suffer simply for the sake of it. Rather, when God brings suffering to us, we persevere and look forward to the maturity it will bring. In the face of suffering, we should ask God for the wisdom to see trials in this light. If we do this, we will not be tempted to grumble, for we will see the true value of trials. We will also understand that the generosity of God extends even to the trials that we face.

Look again at James 1:1-18.

5. In this passage, what is God like (vv. 5, 13, 17, 18)?

6. What were some of the trials that James' readers were facing?

- 1:9-11

- 2:1-7

- 2:15-16

- 4:1-8

- 5:1-6

- 5:8-11

GOD IS GOOD, AND SO ARE ALL HIS gifts—even testings. Understanding the text, however, is only the first step. Putting this into practice when we face trials is much more difficult. We need to pray that God will give us this wisdom so that we will persevere under trials and not grumble, considering it all joy instead.

» Implications

(Choose one or more of the following to think about further or to discuss in your group.)

- Think of a conversation you had today with a friend. How much of the conversation was positive? How much was negative, grumbling about what is wrong with your life or the world?

- You have just had a bad day at work. How do you avoid grumbling to your family/flatmates?

- Consider some examples of meeting trials in a godly fashion by reading these verses:

  - Daniel 3:16-18

  - Acts 5:40-42

  - Acts 16:22-25

  Think about how you might be persecuted for being Christian. How could these examples help your response?

- What is the world's usual way of responding to trials (Rev 16:8-11)?

- What difficulties have you recently faced or are you facing? How might God be using them for your maturity?

» Give thanks and pray

- Thank God for the comfort and reassurance there is in knowing that we can come to him in prayer, confident he will respond generously.
- Pray that God would give you the wisdom to meet the trials you are facing with joy.
- Ask God to deliver you from temptation and sinful desires.

» STUDY 3

JUST DO IT

[JAMES 1:19–27]

BEING A STUDENT IS EASY. WELL, part of it is. When you are a student you learn information from textbooks or classes, and that is the end of it. You do not have to change your life at all. When you learn what Marx says about politics, you do not have to become a Marxist. When you learn how to reinforce concrete, you do not have to go and do it. Whether or not you pass the exam depends only on what knowledge you have in your head, not on how you acted on the way to the exam.

Bible knowledge is very different. For this exam, your entire life counts. You cannot learn it impartially as a body of information. Understanding it properly means that you must live by it. James' overriding concern, which really sums up the whole book, is to see truth in action. In our last study we saw that we must put the Word into action when we are facing trials, not complaining or blaming God, but instead persevering. In this next passage, James wants his readers to understand that truth is not just something you know in your head—it is something you live. We often regard arguments about truth as a matter of intellectual speculation. God's truth, however, is found in action. With God's truth, if you do not live it, you have not really learnt it.

Read James 1:19–27.

1. What has God done for our salvation (vv. 19–21; cf. v. 18)?

2. What should our response be (vv. 19–22)?

Humbly accept the Word

WE ARE SO USED TO HAVING the word of God that we can forget the immense privilege it is. We have been granted access to the secrets of God's mind and his plan for the universe.

It is also easy for us to have an attitude that seeks to argue, not to obey. Our modern society is forever telling us to do what is best for ourselves, to be self-determining, not to accept what others tell us to do. This is a very popular attitude, for it panders to our natural selfishness. No-one really wants to listen in an attitude of obedience. Yet this is the very person God esteems—the one who is humble and contrite in spirit and trembles at his word (Isa 66:2).

This **attitude** is summed up in verse 21: receive God's word "with meekness". God has implanted his saving word in us; the only appropriate response is to meekly receive it. In many ways, this is the key verse of the whole letter. James constantly encourages his readers to have this attitude of humble acceptance of what God says. Our attitude to God's word—whether we submit to it meekly, or not—is the basis for all the specific instructions James gives.

It's your attitude that matters

This doesn't mean that we can never ask questions or seek to explore what God is saying more fully—in fact, his word requires understanding and it is good to explore it deeply. The difference lies in our attitude as we do this. Are we asking questions to try to avoid the meaning of the text, or do we obediently trust that God knows best?

Read James 1:21-27 again.

3. How do we "receive with meekness the implanted word" in practice?

4. What is the deception that James warns against?

5. What is the result of having the right attitude to God's word (v. 25)?

What does it mean to receive the Word meekly?

OBEDIENCE IS CRUCIAL TO understanding the Bible. Merely listening (studying, reading, marking, learning) in Bible study groups is not enough. We must do what it says. That is, we must be humble enough to do things God's way, not our own. Receiving God's word meekly (or humbly) means submitting to it; **it means doing it**. Such submission will affect the very way we read—for if we are keen to do what the Word says, we will be keen to find out what it says. If we are keen to do what we want to do, we will simply try to make the Bible justify our own actions.

Being a doer who acts

One application of 'doing' God's word is in the way we speak to other people. Just as we are to be quick to listen to God, we are ►

also to have this attitude to others. We should not speak quickly in anger to others—we should keep a rein on our tongue. This is particularly relevant to small Bible study groups. We may all be good friends, but if there is a disagreement, it is easy to fall into defending our own point of view, rather than listening to others. By nature, we are all keener to express our own opinion than to understand someone else's. (Just check tonight when you go home how much you remember of what you said today, and how much of what others said. We all treasure our own words before anyone else's.) Next time you find yourself getting hot under the collar at what someone else is saying in the group, try letting them finish their entire argument before answering. Answering in quick anger is bound to be harmful (even if you are right!).

When we fail to do the word of God, we deceive ourselves. We cannot learn the word of God just by reading. It is like trying to set your car alarm just by reading the manual: you have to fiddle with the alarm itself before you understand what the manual is saying. Just reading the Bible will not teach us godliness. Putting it into practice, realizing how hard it is and trying again—this is what teaches us. Yet this is not a burden, for we are obeying the perfect law that gives freedom, which comes from God who gives us every good and perfect gift (1:17, 25).

The danger is that we read the Bible and think we know it all. As James says, this is like looking in the mirror but immediately forgetting what you look like! If we read the Word, we should not walk away unchanged; we should do something.

» Implications

(Choose one or more of the following to think about further or to discuss in your group.)

- What is the opposite of accepting the Word with meekness?

- How would you summarize your own attitude to God's word?

- Do your Bible reading habits need improvement? What are some of the different ways we can read the Bible regularly?

- What steps could you take to make sure you put into practice what you hear or read in the Bible?

- Think of what you were struggling with as a Christian this time last year. Have you made any progress?

- Who are the "orphans and widows" or other lonely or needy people in your congregation? How can you help them?

- In what situations do you find yourself quick to speak and quick to become angry? How can you change your behaviour in these situations?

» Give thanks and pray

- Thank God for the gift of his saving word: his son Jesus.
- Praise God for the work he is doing as he refines us and transforms us to be more like Christ in every way.
- Ask God to help you recognize when you are behaving/speaking in a way that is contrary to his word.
- As you read his word this week, ask for God's help in accepting it humbly.

PUT SOME LIFE IN YOUR FAITH

[JAMES 2]

It was a regular night at church. The band was warming up and people were arriving. Tom was not on the official welcoming team, but as he chatted to some of the kids from the youth group he was also on the lookout for newcomers so he could say a friendly word. He noticed some of the youth group kids sniggering, and smelt a strange smell. As he turned, he saw that a tramp had wandered in from the street. He looked around to see if any of the elders were going to ask him to leave. Then his conscience gave him a guilty jolt—Christians should be welcoming, he remembered. With relief he noticed that the pastor had just walked in. Good, that old fellow can be welcomed now, Tom thought, as he shepherded the youth group away from such an unpleasant influence…

How easy it is to be selective about applying our principles! We can understand the *idea* of loving people, but sometimes we need a strong reminder about being consistent in living it out. James hits us with just this kind of reminder in chapter 2.

Skim over James 1.

1. Write a sentence describing what our attitude should be towards God's word.

Read James 1:22-2:13.

2. What is said about the law (1:25, 2:12)?

3. How is the law summed up (2:8)?

4. How is showing favouritism contradictory to this?

5. What is wrong with treating the rich better than the poor?

6. What should our attitude be towards the rich and the poor? (Also compare 1:9-11.)

7. How can breaking the law at one point mean you have broken all of it?

Showing favouritism

THE WORLD THINKS THAT DISCRIMination is bad because it goes against the 'law' of equality: all humans are equal and should be treated as such. The Bible, however, does not speak in those terms. It speaks of mercy and judgement. When we show discrimination between the rich and the poor we forget that the kingdom is about mercy. We are not to be judges over each other, for we are all judged by the Word. How can I condemn anyone, when I know that I deserve to be condemned too? No, if I really understand the saving word of God then I will seek to forgive and to save others, as God has treated me. If I break the law at even one point—if I judge that someone is inferior just because they are poor—then I have broken all of it, for I have sought to condemn instead of love.

All this follows straight on from what James was saying at the end of chapter 1. We must not merely hear the Word; we must do what it says. To show favouritism is an example of hearing what God says (in this case about us), but then acting in clear contradiction of it. It means we have *not* meekly accepted the Word (1:21); we are not obeying it, but rather we are setting ourselves above it, judging what God says and deciding what we like and what we don't. If we receive the Word humbly, that means doing what it says—*whatever* it says.

In the rest of chapter 2, James continues to teach about the importance of hearing *and* doing.

Read James 2:14–26.

8. How does James describe so-called 'faith' (vv. 14, 17, 26)?

9. What is the point of the illustration in verses 15-16?

10. Can you think of some illustrations of our own failure to have real faith?

11. How does James describe the faith of:

- the demons?

- Abraham?

- Rahab?

So-called 'faith'

THIS PASSAGE HAS CAUSED CON-tention for centuries because of the way in which James emphasizes the need for works in order to be saved. Wait a minute, you say: are we not saved by faith alone? What about the teaching of Paul in Romans and Galatians?

Before we jump to the conclusion that James is contradicting Paul, we need to look carefully at what James is saying. He is talking about 'faith' and 'works', but is he talking about the same thing as Paul? Let's investigate.

Read James 2:14-26 again.

12. Work out what James means by these key words from the verses given. (If you want to check Paul's definitions, see Romans 3:21-4:25.)

	James	Paul
Faith/belief (they are the same word in Greek)	2:18-19	trust, reliance, dependence
Works	2:14-17	works of the Old Testament law

THE BIBLE IS FUNDAMENTALLY A collection of books, not verses. To understand any particular verse we must read it within the flow of its book, and not in isolation.

There is no better example of the importance of this than the exercise we have just done in James 2:14-26. Just taking verse 24 on its own, we might find ourselves with a problem when we compare it with Romans 3:28:

> You see that a person is justified by works and not by faith alone. (Jas 2:24)

> For we hold that one is justified by faith apart from works of the law. (Rom 3:28)

When we read each passage in its entirety, however, we see that the two authors are addressing quite different questions, even though some of the words are the same. James is continuing his emphasis from chapter 1: simply hearing God's word and giving intellectual assent to it counts for very little.

Only those who put the Word into practice—whose faith is expressed in good deeds—have a true and living faith at all.

Paul, on the other hand, is addressing those who seek to justify themselves before God by performing the works of the Old Testament law. He teaches that it is only by putting our trust in God's promise of salvation through Jesus that we can be right with him (that is, justified). Later in Romans, Paul goes on to speak about how this trust in God is expressed in a changed lifestyle (e.g. Romans 6, 8, 12).

John Calvin summarized the relationship between faith and works well: "We are saved by faith alone, but saving faith is never alone". A true saving faith will always be expressed in action, in the good deeds that God has prepared for us to do (cf. Eph 2:8-10). If our response to God's offer of salvation is simply to hear it, or nod our heads in intellectual assent to it, and not *act* upon it, then we have not really put our trust in what we have heard. Our faith is lifeless; dead as a doornail.

» Implications

- Is there anyone in your congregation who is in material need? Is there anyone in your congregation who is not 'your type'—someone you had never thought of talking to? What can you do about it?

- Are there any other areas in your life that are inconsistent with your trust in God?

- You explain to a non-Christian friend that we are not saved by good works but by Jesus' death. You challenge your friend to repent and have faith in Christ. He or she replies that if you are saved just by believing in Jesus, then it does not matter what you do. How would you answer from James?

» Give thanks and pray

- Thank God for the privilege we have of being his representatives on Earth, and for the good deeds he has set aside for us to do in his name.
- Ask God to help you as you struggle to understand and apply the relationship between faith and works.
- Pray for new opportunities to work out your faith in everyday life.
- Thank God that we are not alone, but are part of a family of believers who can spur each other on to love and good deeds.

THE UNCONTROLLABLE TONGUE

[JAMES 3:1-12]

ALL THE STARS WERE THERE, AS the famous Jackson family awarded honours to their friends in the entertainment world. At a poignant moment in her speech, Elizabeth Taylor called upon the general public to stop buying the newspapers of the gutter press. As one who has fuelled such newspapers for years, she was in a position to make such a plea—and those newspapers probably boosted their sales the next day with photographs of her saying so. She was right, however, in perceiving that the tabloids exist not because of particularly evil publishers, but because the public buys them. We just love gossip. We love hearing it, we love spreading it, and we especially love being the first with the news so we can shock others when we tell them.

"If you can't say something nice about a person, don't say anything at all", mother used to say. Wouldn't it be nice if the media did that? Wouldn't it be nice if we did that? If we could only control our tongues, life would be a lot easier for most of us (except for those out-of-work publishers). James recognizes uncontrolled tongues as one of the major causes of distress amongst Christians. Whether we are teachers or not, how can we learn to control our tongues?

Those who teach others about God present a particularly striking example of the problems of the tongue, and it is here that James begins. As the passage proceeds, however, his discussion of the problems of the tongue seems to broaden to include all of us.

Read James 3:1–12.

1. What problems does a teacher face?

2. Why is it so easy to make mistakes as a teacher?

3. What do horses, ships, forest fires and the human body have in common?

4. What do beasts, birds, reptiles, sea creatures and the human tongue not have in common?

5. Is there anyone who can control the tongue?

6. If no man can tame the tongue, do you think verse 10 presents an impossible demand? Why? Why not?

AT FIRST GLANCE, JAMES 3:1-10 presents a fairly depressing picture. First, we are warned to think twice before teaching others, because **those who teach** will be judged more strictly. Presumably, this is because when teachers make mistakes, they hurt not only themselves but also those in their care.

Given the seriousness of this responsibility, teachers have a problem. How are they going to avoid making mistakes in what they say (and incurring judgement) when their tongues always seem to run away from them? The examples of large things controlled by small things (horses, ships, fires) emphasizes just what the teacher—and the rest of us—are up against. The sequence of illustrations builds in intensity, from the relatively easily bridled horse, to the large wind-tossed ship, to the raging forest fire. James seems quite convinced that no-one is able to douse the destructive spark that is the tongue. He paints it as a devilish secret agent in our midst, a traitor that is always handing us over to the enemy.

What hope do we have then? How can the teacher avoid constantly making mistakes? How can all of us avoid the blasphemous hypocrisy of verse 9, where we bless God with one breath and curse the creatures made in his image in the next?

Let us read on.

Read James 3:6–18.

7. What is the point of the illustrations in verses 11-12? Try to write down in your own words what they are teaching about the tongue.

Teachers of the Word

Christian teachers are more than conveyors of ideas: they are leaders by word and life. The best kind of teacher is the one who does not teach subjects, but teaches students. That is, the best teaching (even in a secular context) comes through relationships where the teacher genuinely cares about the students. This kind of effort is even more necessary in Christian teaching, where the teacher is an example of the life he is preaching.

Teachers will be held accountable for the accuracy of their teaching as well as for the life they lead, for true Christian teaching is all about a new way of living. As we saw in chapters 1-2, only those who do the Word have really understood the Word, and so teachers must be far more than conveyors of ideas. To teach the Word, they must understand it; and if they have understood it, they will live changed lives, lives of obedience and good works. This is a dread responsibility, and one not to be undertaken lightly, says James.

8. How is true wisdom shown?

9. Compare Jesus' teaching in Matthew 12:33-37. How does it throw light on this passage?

10. In terms of our speech, how can we make sure that what comes out of our mouths is 'fresh water' and not 'salt water'?

Matters of the heart

When we tell a lie about why we were late for an appointment, or why we didn't phone someone back when we said we would, what is going on in our hearts? We want to avoid looking bad. Our pride in this situation is more powerful than our love of the truth. We would rather lie and preserve our respectability than tell the truth and go down a notch or two in the eyes of others.

If we are having trouble with our tongues, we need to go back and look at the spring from which the water flows. We need to repent, to draw near to God and ask him to transform us from the inside out.

As WE SHALL SEE IN OUR next study, in chapters 3-4 James is particularly concerned about the double-minded Christian. Indeed, this has been his concern throughout the letter. He wants his readers to humbly accept the Word planted in them, and to demonstrate this by constantly living it out. In the rest of chapter 3, he relates this to the chasm that exists between God's true wisdom (and the peace that it brings) and the demonic counterfeit that breeds only ambition and jealousy. Regardless of what we claim, the kind of wisdom we really possess will be revealed by our actions (whether peace and good deeds, or envy and discord). This is like the spring of water in verses 11-12. The output depends on what is at the source.

This helps us as we think about our tongues and how to deal with them. Jesus says that "out of the abundance of the heart [the] mouth speaks" (Luke 6:45). Even if we can never completely control our tongues, we can do something about **our hearts**. We can quit being double-minded or compromised in our allegiances. We can flee the devil and draw near to our Father. We can pray for the pure and peaceable wisdom that comes down from above. (More on this in our next study.)

» Implications

(Choose one or more of the following to think about further or to discuss in your group.)

- What recent situations can you think of where your speech has been harmful or has got you into trouble? What attitudes ('heart problems') gave rise to this speech?

- Your Christian friend has just told everyone something you said in private. You are very hurt and think that was an unloving and un-Christian thing to do. Your friend obviously thinks it was not important. Think of the practical steps you would take to resolve the issue and control your tongue in your pain and anger.

- When are you most tempted to slander other people? What is the underlying problem and what can you do about it?

- Are there particular situations in which you have misled or wronged someone with your tongue? What do you need to do to redress this?

- Read 2:12-13 and 4:11-12. How will this motivate you to seek to control your tongue?

» Give thanks and pray

- Thank God that he desires to change us, and that he responds with loving forgiveness when we repent and draw near to him.
- Ask God to forgive you for any sinful and hurtful things you have said recently.
- Ask God for a renewed spirit of self-control as you practise being slow to speak.
- Pray for teachers of God's word: ask God to protect them from bitter jealousy and selfish ambition, and to give them his wisdom. Pray the same for yourself.

THE FIGHT

[JAMES 3:13–4:12]

HAVE YOU EVER EXPERIENCED A public fight in your congregation? There is nothing more ugly and more basically contradictory than Christians fighting amongst themselves. It goes against the very nature of being Christian. "By this all people will know that you are my disciples," said Jesus, "if you have love for one another" (John 13:35). When Christians fight we are denying the very thing that is meant to mark us out as distinctive.

However, the Christians in the congregation to which James wrote were fighting, and James was severely disturbed by it. "What causes quarrels and what causes fights among you?" he asks. How can it be that these people claim to be the people of God, the people who love one another, and yet they are destroying their fellowship through quarrels and fights?

As in our last study, this destructive behaviour is the symptom of an underlying problem. Just as the mouth reveals the state of the heart, so do our actions. Here, the state of the heart is divided. As the passage unfolds, James uses three sets of contrasts to challenge his readers about where their loyalties lie. He talks about two conflicting wisdoms, two incompatible friendships, and ultimately two rival masters. As we shall see, the real problem for James' readers, and the one underlying their fights and quarrels, is their double-mindedness, their inability to turn away from the world and the devil, and to submit to God. They are failing to receive the word of God meekly and obey it, as James said in 1:21-22.

1. Before you read the passage, how would you define wisdom? Think of someone whom you would describe as wise. What makes them so in your eyes?

Read James 3:13–4:3.

2. How is real wisdom revealed?

3. Fill out the table below.

	False wisdom	True wisdom
Where it comes from		
Its character		
Its results		

4. How does each kind of wisdom affect the level of peace or discord in a congregation?

5. Does all this alter your definition of wisdom (from question 1)? If so, in what way?

Two wisdoms

IT SEEMS THAT ALTHOUGH SOME OF James' readers were claiming to be wise, they had understood very little about how to recognize true wisdom.

It is not a matter of intelligence, or of quantity of knowledge. It is not about eloquence or persuasiveness. It may even be considered foolish and weak by those looking on (cf. 1 Cor 1:18-25). It comes from above, and consists of a right understanding of God, ourselves and others—an understanding that is inevitably revealed in good deeds done in meekness. True wisdom will always be revealed by humility, gentleness, mercy, and peacemaking, for if we truly perceive the greatness of God, our own sinfulness, and the love that he has shown towards us, then envy, ambition and hostility can have no place.

Read James 4:1-10.

6. What do their fights and ineffective prayers have in common?

A note on translation

In the NIV, the word translated 'desires' in verse 1 is the same Greek word as the word translated 'pleasures' in verse 3. The word is translated as 'passions' in the ESV in both verses.

7. Carefully re-read verses 3-4. What does it means to be motivated by our passions?

8. Why would James describe this as adultery?

9. In verses 6-10:

- What is demanded of us?

- What is promised to us?

10. Describe, in your own words, the basic problem that James is addressing.

Two wisdoms, two friendships

ACCORDING TO JAMES, THE CHRIS-tian is always faced with a choice. It is the same sort of choice Elijah laid before the Israelites on Mt Carmel:

> "How long will you go limping between two different opinions? If the LORD is God, follow him; but if Baal, then follow him." (1 Kgs 18:21)

The choice we constantly face comes to us in different forms and guises: the passions or pleasures that are at war within ourselves (in verses 1 and 3); the seductive world of verse 4, which tries to win our friendship; and the devil of verse 7, who must be resisted. The battle is waged on these three fronts, but it is the same battle and the same choice—the choice for or against God. We cannot serve two masters.

Sometimes it seems as if we can serve two masters. After all, we still have non-Christian friends; we still need a house to live in; we still need money to live on. Of course we do, and all those things are good—as long as we keep them in their place. In the end, we have to ask ourselves whether our involvement with the world is simply a vehicle for our own desires for acceptance, status, power and comfort, or whether we are serving God. It is impossible to do both.

God requires that we abandon our double-mindedness, that we quit trying to have a foot in both camps. Yet he also promises us a great power: if we resist the devil, he will flee. God promises grace to those who submit to him, who humbly accept his word and obey it. We can choose to serve God; we are not locked into a lifelong dismal cycle of sin.

This knowledge is both a comfort and a challenge. It is a comfort, for we know that we do have the power to resist sin; it is a challenge, for if God gives us the capacity to resist sin, we must take this seriously and do so.

It is only by resolving our mixed loyalties, and humbling ourselves before our true master and his word, that the surface problems of fighting, quarrelling, envy and ineffective prayer will be dealt with. In seeing the necessity of that choice, in making that choice for God, and in seeing the good fruits that follow from it—there lies true wisdom.

» Implications

(Choose one or more of the following to think about further or to discuss in your group.)

- How can we humble ourselves before God? What does that mean in practice (cf. 1:18-22)?

- Are you growing in wisdom? What signs are there in your life?

- In what ways do you see your Christian life being compromised by:

  - your own desires and passions?

  - the influence of the world?

- Your church council has just announced that they consider many modern Christian songs unhelpful, so from now on no contemporary songs at all will be sung in church. You are furious. You point out all the good ones that exist, but they do not listen. The youth group are thoroughly turned off church and stop volunteering to help with the music. What are you going to do?

- What changes are you going to make to your prayer life in response to this study?

» Give thanks and pray

- Thank God for the comfort of knowing that when we come near to him he promises to come near to us.
- Ask God to help you as you struggle with living in the world and not being of the world (John 15:19). Ask God to take away your double-mindedness.
- Thank him for the promise of the life that is to come when we leave this world: an eternity worshipping Jesus.
- Pray that you would be considerate and loving peacemakers who sow in peace.

WEALTH AND POVERTY

[JAMES 4:13–5:11]

MONEY IS DIFFICULT STUFF TO handle. If you have it, you are tempted to be arrogant; if you do not have it, you are tempted to grumble and be discontent. Rich or poor, we are all tempted to greed, and a disparity in wages is something difficult to overcome in Christian relationships.

We have already seen that James' readers were troubled by quarrels, grumbling and discontent. Their grumbling was especially over their posses-sions—it seems that the haves and the have-nots could not get on. They were torn by favouritism and gossip, the rich looking down on the poor and the poor muttering against the rich. They were all guilty of being judgemental, forgetting the Word that had saved them.

In 4:13 and 5:1 we have two para-graphs starting "Come now". James has something important to say and he wants these quarrelling, slanderous people to take note.

Read James 4:13–17.

1. Who needs to pay attention (v. 13)?

2. How is their behaviour inconsistent with the truth?

3. What should their attitude to the future be?

Read James 5:1–6.

4. Who needs to pay attention (v. 1)?

5. What have they done?

6. What does the future hold for them?

WE WHO ARE WEALTHY ARE USED TO buying, travelling and organizing. We assume it is our right to do so. We make our business decisions and our travel plans as if we are in control, for we feel as if we *are* in control. We forget that it is only by God's will that our plans are carried out. Our wealth could disappear overnight—we could have an accident, lose the ability to work, even lose our lives—and all our plans would come to nothing. In the freedom of being rich, we must still remember that God is in control, not us (cf. Prov 16:9; 19:21).

The wealthy must also beware of the corruption and fraud that so often is associated with wealth. Money in itself is good; but our hearts are wicked, and rich people can be tempted to seek to gain even more than they already have, through dishonesty and oppression of the poor (as our world shows only too frequently). We must not idolize wealth by seeking favours of the wealthy in our churches or society. The glamour can too easily blind us to the possibilities for corruption.

Now we turn to James' warnings to the poor.

Read James 5:7–11.

7. Who is addressed in verses 7 and 10?

8. How are they reacting to their situation?

9. What should their basic attitude be?

10. What examples does James give to illustrate this attitude?

11. What does the future hold for them?

12. How is the coming of the Lord related to patience and grumbling?

The materialism of the poor

When money is tight, the natural response is to envy the rich, grumble about oppression, be discontent with what we have and appeal for justice. It is still a warlike attitude, which James is against. It is still double-minded, wanting money for worldly reasons, to be able to compete with the rich. It is still love of money, which 1 Timothy 6:10 tells us is "a root of all kinds of evils".

YOU DO NOT HAVE TO BE RICH to be materialistic. It is easy for the **poor** to grumble, and they sound like they have a genuine grievance (which indeed they may). James warns that this is not a godly reaction.

What is wrong with grumbling? Taking us back to a previous theme (see, it is all connected!), grumbling is a misuse of the tongue, and inappropriate for Christians who profess love for one another. Also, it is playing the judge (another previous theme), telling God what he ought to do and putting others down. For the poor to grumble against the rich is as bad as for the rich to discriminate against the poor (cf. 2:4). After all, for all you know, the rich man may be very generous with his money. In other words, just as the rich in their arrogance fail to live in the light of God's sovereignty and his imminent coming, so too may the poor.

Materialism under God

The Bible is not against wealth or pleasure; both are a good part of creation, given to us by God. It is not money that is "a root of all kinds of evils"—it is the *love* of money (1 Tim 6:10), which leads to jealousy and competitiveness. We must enjoy money, using it generously in the same way that God is generous.

James puts this message in the context of judgement, not creation. He urges us to see both wealth and poverty in the light of the end of the world. For both the rich and the poor, the approach of the final day gives us a very different perspective on wealth.

» Implications

(Choose one or more of the following to think about further or to discuss in your group.)

• In what ways do you see the arrogance of the wealthy in our society?

• How are we tempted to idolize wealth?

• How can we guard against idolizing wealth?

- What is good and what is bad about money?

- Why do we possess anything individually? Should we?

- You and your friend are both Christians but he or she has taken on a much more highly-paid job and is gathering the kinds of possessions you wish you had. It seems unfair that a Christian could be so rich. This situation may well last for the rest of your life. How are you going to cope with your friend's wealth?

- "The coming of the Lord is at hand" (5:8). What difference does this make in your attitude towards the things you own now?

» Give thanks and pray

- Thank God for his goodness and for the money he gives us to use wisely.
- Praise him for being a God who is full of compassion and mercy.
- Ask God for patience and perseverance as you wait for the return of Christ.

HOW POWERFUL IS PRAYER?

[JAMES 5:12-20]

WHAT DO YOU DO WHEN YOU'RE sick? Do you go to the doctor, thinking nothing more of it? Do you go to the doctor, thanking God that he provides the medical system? Do you go to a healer who will pray for you? Do you ask your elders to anoint you with oil?

James 5 has been a thorny chapter on the issue of healing. Different churches have taken different attitudes to it, emphasizing different parts of what is written. If you have never had the elders pray over you, why not? Doesn't James tell you to? If you have, and you did not get better, why not? Was the problem with you, the elders, the oil or God's faithfulness?

Perhaps—and this is always more likely—we have simply misunderstood the text. As Bible readers and sinners, we must remember that we are prone to distort and disbelieve what is on the page in front of us. That is why we must always check what we are told (even in these studies!) against the text itself, and work hard to see what is really written there, not what we want to read into it. For this reason, this study is a little different from the others in the book—it has more explanatory notes than usual. A tricky passage such as James 5:12-20 requires a little more work to tease out the meaning, so please take the time to consider the notes and study the Bible text carefully.

Because James is not disjointed, but a coherent letter with connecting themes, we must read any part of it in the context of the whole letter. Here in chapter 5 we have a passage very frequently taken out of context and read as if it were simply a short list of instructions on its own. It is especially easy to take it out of context if you believe James is just snippets of advice which stand alone.

However, we have seen that James is not like that; the whole letter holds together. It is based on the key idea of 1:21-22, which is that we should receive the word of God with meekness and so do what it says, not judging or quarrelling between ourselves. The letter starts and ends with prayer—a correct response to tribulation. We have seen that prayers are ineffective when we have worldly hearts; and that we are in the habit of misusing our tongues, cursing instead of praising.

In James 5:12, then, James' instruction against the misuse of the tongue continues. Do not swear, he says. Be in control of your tongue. Say what you mean, and be a person of your word. If you are suffering, do not swear curses for this is an inappropriate use of the tongue.

Read James 5:12–20.

1. What is the appropriate response in trouble?

2. What is the appropriate response in happiness?

3. What makes both of these responses difficult?

4. What should we do in sickness?

5. What will be the result for the sick person (v. 15)?

6. What should the whole congregation do (v. 16)?

THIS PASSAGE CERTAINLY SEEMS to present us with a great promise. The sick person will be healed, James says. He will be raised up and forgiven. The example of Elijah is very striking—it shows what great power there is in prayer. Elijah prayed and a drought came, and then he prayed and brought rain. If we are to take this passage seriously, then we should pray expectantly. Why then is there so little healing taking place today? Why does this not work? Indeed, why did James himself die? If this promise is true, why do Christians die at all? James promises that if we follow these instructions, prayer is so powerful that we will be healed. What is this passage saying?

We can have various different responses at this point.

(i) We can lose confidence in the power of prayer and, as a result, modify the promise: you cannot really pray for healing; you can only pray for acceptance of sickness.

Misinterpretations

Two ways of interpreting this passage have been particularly influential. The first one is the Roman Catholic sacrament of the Last Rites, or Extreme Unction. A person on his or her deathbed is visited by a priest and says confession. The priest anoints the person with oil and prays, in the belief that the person will thereby be forgiven his or her sins and go to heaven.

The second is the Charismatic use of this passage as the basis for healing services. At the healing service someone ▶

believed to have the gift of healing lays hands on the sick person, trusting that the sick person will be healed physically, according to the promise of this passage.

Each of these interpretations has (at least) superficial problems. First of all, for the Catholic reading, James says the sick person is going to be healed. But administering Extreme Unction on the person's deathbed assumes the person is not going to get well. (Historically this sacrament was used as a healing ritual for any sick person, but during the Middle Ages it developed into a deathbed service.) Also, the passage says to confess to each other, not to a priest.

The Charismatic reading also has some problems. James does not talk about a healing service; what is described in 5:14-16 sounds like a private meeting. Also, the sick person is to call the elders—the regular leaders and teachers of the church—not someone with the gift of healing. A question also has to be raised about the connection between sin and healing in the Charismatic reading. If the person is not healed, does that mean he or she is still sinful?

(ii) We can move into fantasy land and claim that healings have taken place which really have not. Many people have done this, to their cost. The problem is not solved by shutting our eyes to reality.

(iii) We can add qualifications: you need to pray in faith, and without faith it will not work; or maybe the oil really stands for medicine; or maybe you have to pray in the name of the Lord; or maybe it is not his will for the person to be healed.

None of these are really satisfactory. If this passage truly promises healing, then the continued illness of Christians raises problems for our belief in the Bible. Now it is time to look more closely at the passage and its context.

Read James 5:13–20 again.

7. Do you notice anything odd or unusual in the wording of this passage? Does anything strike you as surprising?

8. Compare the wording of these two different translations. What differences are there?

English Standard Version:
v. 15 And the prayer of faith will save the one who is sick, and the Lord will raise him up. And if he has committed sins, he will be forgiven.
v. 16 Therefore, confess your sins to one another and pray for one another, that you may be healed. The prayer of a righteous person has great power as it is working.

New International Version:
v. 15 And the prayer offered in faith will make the sick person well; the Lord will raise him up. If he has sinned, he will be forgiven.
v. 16 Therefore confess your sins to each other and pray for each other so that you may be healed. The prayer of a righteous man is powerful and effective.

THE ENGLISH STANDARD VERSION actually reflects the original Greek more closely. What the text really says is that the sick person will be *saved*. Of course, that could easily mean 'saved from sickness'—that is, healed; that is why the NIV translators have said "make the sick person well". However, strictly speaking, we have this odd situation where the sick person is going to be saved (v. 15), and the sinner healed (v. 16). Why not the other way around?

Let us unravel this passage starting, with the relevance of Elijah.

By Elijah's prayer, a drought came to Israel as God's punishment for Israel's sin. By his prayer again, rain came as a sign of Israel being restored to relationship with God. Elijah's ministry was precisely what James 5:19-20 speaks of—to bring back the sinful nation and cover a multitude of sins, thereby saving people. (To see this for yourself, look up 1 Kings 17-2 Kings 2. There will probably not be time for you to do this in your group.)

Although we all suffer sickness generally and indiscriminately as a result of Adam's sin, there are also cases when God sends specific sickness to a congregation for the sin of its members (as 1 Corinthians 11:27-32 shows).

This helps us to read James 5:12-20

Sickness and sin

This passage should jolt us in our beliefs about prayer and sin. It is so easy to be blasé about the power and importance of both.

Sin is serious, and can bring sickness. In our technological arrogance, we assume physical ills are independent of our spiritual state, and independently curable. This is not the case. There is some sickness which comes directly from God as a result of sin. Indeed, we should never lose sight of the fact that all sickness comes from God as the result of humankind's rejection of him. Sickness is a warning about the coming judgement.

If you are sick, it is right to think about your sin; if there is a sin on your conscience, confess it and pray. You may or may not be healed, for you do not know what was the cause of that particular sickness. However, you will have taken God more seriously, which is what James challenges us to do.

We must also remember that when Christians are in rebellion against God, we must take it seriously and *expect* God's warning and discipline through sickness. Just as the God of Elijah sent drought to punish sin, so he may punish our sin directly now. God loves us and offers great mercy. We must not take that for granted, for the sin he is forgiving is great.

in a different light. The congregation is sinning, as we have seen: they are judging between themselves, grumbling, and so on. It is natural for James to ask: Is anyone sick? If so, they need to confess and the elders need to pray, for it is possible that the **sickness is a result of sin**. This is why the sick person is instructed to call the elders, not the doctors. We *can* have healing through prayer, and if the judgement of God is upon us for some particular sin then we should pray.

Ah, you ask the burning question. How do I know if my sickness is a result of sin, and not just the general sickness of the world? This is a good question. The godly person who falls sick *will* ask first—is this a judgement on me? Sickness should be a cause for examining the conscience. When you find sin, and especially if you find particular unrepented sin, you should pray for forgiveness. If the sickness *was* a punishment for sin, James promises us you will be healed.

Did you notice that one of the oddities of verse 15 is that James says "*if* he has committed sins"? Of course he has sinned—everyone sins. James is asking if there is any *particular* sin which might be the cause of the illness.

Your sickness, however, may not be a result of specific sin. In that case, you may not be healed; but whatever sin was on your conscience (and there is bound to be something) will be forgiven, through confession and prayer. You may still be sick; but you will have dealt with the sin, which, after all, is more important.

» Implications

(Choose one or more of the following to think about further or to discuss in your group.)

- How can we save people?

- What is the connection between sickness and sin?

- Is sickness sent to us when we commit individual sins? What do the following passages reveal?

  - John 9:1–3

  - Mark 2:5

- 1 Corinthians 11:27-32

- John 5:14

- Describe the steps you would go through, in response to this passage, if you suddenly found yourself ill.

- Is your congregation fighting or unloving, or is any member obviously involved in sin? What can you do about it?

- Are you involved in sin? What will you do about it?

- When you are sick, do you examine your conscience for sin? How can you make sure this is a godly response and not a morbid obsession?

- Have you worked out how you can love the other Christians in your congregation? Think of a practical program for yourself: it may be inviting church members home for a meal, making sure you talk to at least one new person each week, or aiming to meet one new person and looking after them. What can you do?

- What has this passage taught you about prayer?

» Give thanks and pray

- Thank God for the forgiveness he offers us. Ask him to help us not to take it for granted.
- Spend some time in prayer for people you know who are sick or struggling with unrepentant sinful behaviours; pray that they may be saved and healed.
- Ask for God's help and wisdom as you strive to meekly receive his word and apply it in your daily life.

Feedback on this resource

We really appreciate getting feedback about our resources—not just suggestions for how to improve them, but also positive feedback and ways they can be used. We especially love to hear that the resources may have helped someone in their Christian growth.

You can send feedback to us via the 'Feedback' menu in our online store, or write to us at info@matthiasmedia.com.au.

❀matthiasmedia

Matthias Media is an evangelical publishing ministry that seeks to persuade all Christians of the truth of God's purposes in Jesus Christ as revealed in the Bible, and equip them with high-quality resources, so that by the work of the Holy Spirit they will:

- abandon their lives to the honour and service of Christ in daily holiness and decision-making
- pray constantly in Christ's name for the fruitfulness and growth of his gospel
- speak the Bible's life-changing word whenever and however they can—in the home, in the world and in the fellowship of his people.

Our wide range of resources includes Bible studies, books, training courses, tracts and children's material. To find out more, and to access samples and free downloads, visit our website:

www.matthiasmedia.com

How to buy our resources

1. Direct from us over the internet:
   – in the US: www.matthiasmedia.com
   – in Australia: www.matthiasmedia.com.au

2. Direct from us by phone: please visit our website for current phone contact information.

3. Through a range of outlets in various parts of the world. Visit **www.matthiasmedia.com/contact** for details about recommended retailers in your part of the world.

4. Trade enquiries can be addressed to:
   – in the US and Canada: sales@matthiasmedia.com
   – in Australia and the rest of the world: sales@matthiasmedia.com.au

For more resources by Phillip Jensen, visit phillipjensen.com.

Other Interactive and Topical Bible Studies from Matthias Media

Our Interactive Bible Studies (IBS) and Topical Bible Studies (TBS) are a valuable resource to help you keep feeding from God's word. The IBS series works through passages and books of the Bible; the TBS series pulls together the Bible's teaching on topics such as money or prayer. As of May 2020, the series contains the following titles:

Beyond Eden
GENESIS 1-11
Authors: Phillip Jensen and Tony Payne, 9 studies

Salvation Revealed
GENESIS 12-50
Author: Matt Olliffe, 10 studies

Out of Darkness
EXODUS 1-18
Author: Andrew Reid, 8 studies

The Shadow of Glory
EXODUS 19-40
Author: Andrew Reid, 7 studies

The One and Only
DEUTERONOMY
Author: Bryson Smith, 8 studies

Remember the Rock
JOSHUA
Author: Phil Campbell, 6 studies

The Good, the Bad and the Ugly
JUDGES
Author: Mark Baddeley, 10 studies

Famine and Fortune
RUTH
Authors: Barry Webb and David Höhne, 4 studies

God Will Have His King
1 SAMUEL
Author: Des Smith, 9 studies

Renovator's Dream
NEHEMIAH
Authors: Phil Campbell and Greg Clarke, 7 studies

The Eye of the Storm
JOB
Author: Bryson Smith, 6 studies

The Beginning of Wisdom
PROVERBS VOLUME 1
Author: Joshua Ng, 7 studies

Living the Good Life
PROVERBS VOLUME 2
Author: Joshua Ng, 8 studies

The Search for Meaning
ECCLESIASTES
Author: Tim McMahon, 9 studies

Garden of Love
SONG OF SONGS
Author: Des Smith, 4 studies

Two Cities
ISAIAH
Authors: Andrew Reid and Karen Morris, 9 studies

Kingdom of Dreams
DANIEL
Authors: Andrew Reid and Karen Morris, 9 studies

Burning Desire
OBADIAH AND MALACHI
Authors: Phillip Jensen and Richard Pulley, 6 studies

Warning Signs
JONAH
Author: Andrew Reid, 6 studies

Living by Faith
HABAKKUK
Author: Ian Carmichael, 5 studies

On That Day
ZECHARIAH
Author: Tim McMahon, 8 studies

Full of Promise
O.T. OVERVIEW
Authors: Phil Campbell and Bryson Smith, 8 studies

The Good Living Guide
MATTHEW 5:1-12
Authors: Phillip Jensen and Tony Payne, 9 studies

News of the Hour
MARK
Authors: Peter Bolt and Tony Payne, 10 studies

Proclaiming the Risen Lord
LUKE 24-ACTS 2
Author: Peter Bolt, 6 studies

Introducing Jesus
JOHN 1-4
Author: Matt Olliffe, 9 studies

Challenging Jesus
JOHN 5-12
Author: Matt Olliffe, 10 studies

Mission Unstoppable
ACTS
Author: Bryson Smith, 10 studies

The Free Gift of Life
ROMANS 1-5
Author: Gordon Cheng, 8 studies

The Free Gift of Sonship
ROMANS 6-11
Author: Gordon Cheng, 8 studies

The Freedom of Christian Living
ROMANS 12-16
Author: Gordon Cheng, 7 studies

Free for All
GALATIANS
Authors: Phillip Jensen and Kel Richards, 8 studies

Walk this Way
EPHESIANS
Author: Bryson Smith, 8 studies

Partners for Life
PHILIPPIANS
Author: Tim Thorburn, 8 studies

The Complete Christian
COLOSSIANS
Authors: Phillip Jensen and Tony Payne, 8 studies

To the Householder
1 TIMOTHY
Authors: Phillip Jensen and Greg Clarke, 9 studies

Run the Race
2 TIMOTHY
Author: Bryson Smith, 6 studies

The Path to Godliness
TITUS
Authors: Phillip Jensen and Tony Payne, 7 studies

From Shadow to Reality
HEBREWS
Author: Joshua Ng, 10 studies

The Implanted Word
JAMES
Authors: Phillip Jensen and Kirsten Birkett, 8 studies

Homeward Bound
1 PETER
Authors: Phillip Jensen and Tony Payne, 10 studies

All You Need to Know
2 PETER
Author: Bryson Smith, 6 studies

Rest Assured
1 JOHN
Author: Bryson Smith, 9 studies

The Vision Statement
REVELATION
Author: Greg Clarke, 9 studies

The Blueprint
DOCTRINE
Authors: Phillip Jensen and Tony Payne, 9 studies

Bold I Approach
PRAYER
Author: Tony Payne, 6 studies

Cash Values
MONEY
Author: Tony Payne, 5 studies

Sing for Joy
SINGING IN CHURCH
Author: Nathan Lovell, 6 studies

Woman of God
THE BIBLE ON WOMEN
Author: Terry Blowes, 8 studies

GoThereFor.com

Have you ever found yourself in the following situations?

- Your Bible study has decided they want to start studying Ephesians... tomorrow.
- Your colleague has agreed to investigate the Bible with you, but you don't know where to start.
- You forgot to order your new Bible reading material in time.
- A family member has asked you why a good God allows suffering, and you're not sure how to answer them.

GoThereFor.com is an online library that provides you with essential ministry materials, instantly. Subscribe and download what you need, when you need it, and give your friends a digital copy (or print it for them) so they can use it with you.

No postage costs and waiting periods. No limit to the number of studies you can use. No need to clean scratches off a DVD. Just great Bible studies, personal Bible reading material, training courses, videos and ebooks.

Visit **www.gotherefor.com/join** for subscription information.

Digital ideas and resources for real-life ministry